What's Your Style?

Alison Bell

fearless Fashion

Lobster Press™

Fearless Fashion
Text © 2004 Alison Bell

Published by Lobster Press™
1620 Sherbrooke Street West, Suites C & D
Montréal, Québec H3H 1C9
Tel. (514) 904-1100 • Fax (514) 904-1101
www.lobsterpress.com

Publisher: Alison Fripp
Editors: Alison Fripp & Karen Li
Illustrations: Jérôme Mireault, colagene.com
Cover & Book Design: Olena Lytvyn
Production Manager: Tammy Desnoyers

We acknowledge the financial support of the Government of Canada through the Book Publishing Industry Development Program (BPIDP) for our publishing activities.

The Canada Council | Le Conseil des Arts
for the Arts | du Canada

We acknowledge the support of the Canada Council for the Arts for our publishing program.

National Library of Canada Cataloguing in Publication

Bell, Alison
    Fearless fashion / by Alison Bell.

ISBN 1-894222-86-5

    1. Fashion--Juvenile literature. 2. Clothing and dress--Juvenile literature. I. Title.

GT518.B45 2004   j391   C2004-901478-1

Printed and bound in India.

TABLE OF *Contents*

To my amazing daughter Libby—may you remain fearless forever.
—Alison BELL

Introduction

STYLE. What is it? Who has it? And why is it so important to our lives?

THE TRUTH IS, when we look good, we feel good. Pull the right outfit out of your closet and the day goes by without a hitch. Birds chirp, you ace your English exam, and the guy that you've been noticing seems to notice you right back. Put on something that makes you feel self-conscious and the day can quickly go down the drain.

It's not a matter of luck. Style is an expression of self-confidence. If you aren't comfortable with what you're wearing, you'll be tugging and slouching and sending out signals that you'd rather not be seen. On the other hand, putting on your favorite pair of jeans, or that sweater that makes your eyes just pop, will have you standing straight and smiling large.

Style is also a matter of trends: what looks cool, and who is wearing it? *What's Your Style: Fearless Fashion* will give you the lowdown and the background on all the hottest looks of the season. Take our style quiz to discover your true fashion personality, then follow us through seven different trends to find the perfect mix for you. With so much choice, there's no question of ever being out of style; the only thing left to consider is how to satisfy the cravings of your inner Fashionista.

WHAT'S *Your* STYLE?

WHETHER you're a punk, a skater girl, or a total prep, your clothes are an important expression of your personality. In turn, your lifestyle choices will also influence the way you dress. So who is the essential fashion you?

Take this quiz to find out

1. A friend just got a belly button ring. You'll be getting one ...

a. Right after you schedule that elective root canal—never!

b. You can't believe your buddy beat you to it. You're getting one ASAP.

c. You're not sure. There must be a more interesting place to pierce.

d. Maybe one day if you're in the right place at the right time.

2. You usually wear your hair...

a. Neatly combed with a classic cut.

b. Full of mousse, gel, and maybe an extension or two.

c. Whatever style other girls aren't wearing.

d. In a ponytail.

3. You're going out to a party. How long will it take you to get ready?

a. 10–15 minutes, max! Your wardrobe is pretty simple and mixes well, so you don't have to agonize over what to wear.

b. At least an hour, maybe longer. You need to try on at least five outfits to nail down the right look.

c. It all depends on how fast you can pull together an eclectic outfit that will really stand out.

d. No time at all. You may not even change from what you're already wearing.

4. If you were stranded on a deserted island, which of the following would you want to bring with you?

a. Long-wearing, always-stylish staples: white tees, khaki shorts.

b. Your entire closet, accessories included. Hey, even an island girl's gotta look her best.

c. Nothing but your nose ring. Who needs clothing on a deserted island?

d. A swim suit and volleyball.

5. When it comes to makeup, your look is ...

a. Pretty basic: You usually wear a cover-up, neutral lipstick, and a touch of mascara.

b. Wild and fun: You go for bright colors and body glitter.

c. Eyebrow raising: Red lips and a super pale complexion.

d. Barely there: Sometimes you put on lip gloss—if you can remember!

6. Your favorite place to shop for clothes is ...

a. Abercrombie & Fitch or J.Crew.

b. Urban Outfitter.

c. Hot Topic.

d. A skate, surf, or sporting goods store.

7. You and your gal pals are going out to the movies. If you could pick the flick to watch, it would be something like ...

a. The classic "Casablanca."

b. The latest "American Pie."

c. The outlandish "Rocky Horror Picture Show."

d. The adrenaline-pumping "Step Into Liquid."

8 Of the following choices, your friends would probably best describe you as ... (be honest)

a. Reliable and realistic.

b. A trendsetter.

c. Ultra-individualistic.

d. Laid back and easy going.

9 When it comes to showing skin you...

a. Feel comfortable with about an inch or so of your tummy being exposed.

b. Live by the rule, skin is in. The more you can show, the better!

c. Are unpredictable, showing a lot one week, covering up the next.

d. Don't think it's much of an issue with your baggy Ts.

10 The one item of clothing or accessory you'd hate to ever be without:

a. A polo shirt.

b. Just one item?!

c. Fishnet stockings

d. A terry hoody.

How did you score?

If you answered most **a**s, you're a

timeless gal

You are all about a clean and classic look that never goes out of style. Everything about you signals "girl next door." Not to say you're boring. You're not afraid to mix it up a bit and pair a basic T with a studded belt, or wear a shirt with a band logo now and then to add some spice to your outfits. But the best thing about dressing this way is you don't have to think too much. You can jet out the door in a white shirt and pair of boot-cut jeans, and look and feel your best.

If you answered most **b**s, you're

totally trendy

With your nose buried in a fashion magazine, you grab each trend as soon as you see Avril, Gwen, or Britney put it on. You can easily move between different looks, depending on what's hot at the moment. One month, you're totally into the retro look, picking elements from the past, the next, you're adding punk or preppy elements to your wardrobe. Looking great comes naturally to a fashion chameleon like you.

If you answered most **c**s, you're

gotta be me girl

You've got a style all your own. While other kids flock to the mall, you can be found poking around vintage shops or second-hand stores. You love to mix and match patterns or colors and go for outlandish accessories that most kids would never look at. And if something you're wearing does become trendy, that's when you know to kiss it goodbye. One thing you'll always be is one step ahead of the pack!

If you answered most **d**s, you're a

sporty babe

Feeling comfy and casual is everything to you. You can't get enough of sweats, hoodies, rugby shirts, and padded tennis shoes. You've even been known to rob your brother's T-shirt drawer now and then. But it's not as if you haven't put any thought into your look, you just don't understand why other girls spend so much time primping and fussing. Don't they know the natural look is the only way to go?

FASHION 101

Chapter 2

HOWEVER YOU DRESS, it's a far cry from what your mom, grandmother, or great-great grandmother wore.

Throughout history, each era has created its own look that reflected the lifestyle, attitudes, and morals of the time. Nonetheless, one thing has always been true: Whatever the year, women have always wanted to look their best—even if "being fashionable" meant wearing a replica of a battleship on your head or sucking in your waist with a rib-crunching corset made out of whalebone!

Take a peek at some of the most fashionable trends that have popped up through-out the ages, and be glad you live in this millennium!

Stone Age STYLE

ARTIFACTS unearthed in Europe dating as far back as 40,000 B.C. indicate that primitive women made clothes of leaves and grass and covered their heads with bands of feather and bits of rocks and shells. They also decorated their bodies with paint made from plant stains and other natural dyes.

During the Ice Age (40,000–10,000 B.C.) ancient people wrapped themselves in animal skins and furs and even made shirts and other items of clothing by punching holes in the fur with a bone for a needle and sewing up the sides with reindeer sinew. Cave paintings in Europe show pictures of women wearing long bell-shaped fur or skin skirts—the precursor to that mini hanging in your closet.

Ancient ELEGANCE

IN ANCIENT EGYPT (3,000–1,000 B.C.), women wore tight, long dresses made out of linen that sometimes left their breasts bare. They shaved their heads and instead wore wigs made out of human hair. Egyptian gals also knew a thing or two about beauty. They lined their eyes with kohl, painted their lips with a mixture of red ochre and fat, and doused themselves with perfumed oils.

The ancient Greeks went for comfort. Women wore what's called a chiton—a large rectangular piece of wool they draped over their bodies and fastened to their shoulders with brooches and pins and belted at the waist. Over the chiton, they wore a cloak called a himation. As for footwear, they wore sandals or went barefoot."

Medieval TIMES

IN THE 15TH CENTURY, women of the wealthy classes wore loose-flowing gowns with skintight bodices that were belted right below their breasts, giving them a perennial pregnant look. The sleeves of their gowns widened at either the elbow or the wrist and fell trumpet-like over their hands. Some sleeves reached all the way down to the floor. It's obvious that these were not the fashions of the working classes—can you imagine what a fire hazard cooking would have been?

THE Elizabethan ERA

QUEEN ELIZABETH I, who ruled England from 1558 to 1603, was the first international fashion maven. She owned thousands of gowns, and women (as well as men) throughout Europe copied her style. Her most famous fashion contribution is perhaps the popularization of the "ruff." This was a stiff, pleated neck-piece that reached up to the chin, giving women a stern, "head on a platter" look.

Queen Elizabeth's dresses were elaborate and extravagant, mirroring the prosperity of her age. She painted her face white using a mixture of lead and vinegar, which set off a craze in her country. She also shaved her hairline to make her forehead look bigger—another hot look of the 1500s.

get a whiff of this !

Soap and water were out in the 15th- and 16th-century because people thought bathing was hazardous to their health. They believed the water would seep into their skin's pores and give them diseases, such as the Bubonic Plague. So instead of lathering up, they rubbed themselves with dry towels and changed their clothes often. In the 18th century, women concealed dirt with makeup and used perfume to cover up any B.O. Wonder if it worked?

Photo courtesy of N. Davis and M. Schuessler

18th Century CHIC

You hear a lot about Jennifer Lopez's fab buns, but she had nothing on the ladies of yesteryear when they wore a bustle. A bustle was a large padded cushion or a wire or whalebone contraption, which went in and out of fashion between the 1770s–1890s, that women tied around their waists to emphasize their rear ends. Talk about a big booty! Sometimes the bustles would slip out of place, making women look lopsided. And sitting down was far from easy.

THE ARISTOCRATIC LADIES of this era wore at least six layers of clothing, including a chemise (undershirt), corset, petticoat, and a hoop skirt so wide they had to turn sideways to fit through a door. On the plus side, they could actually use their skirts as arm rests.

The mid-to-late 1700s saw the "rise" of towering wigs built over horsehair pads or wire cages. These wigs were cemented into place with animal grease and then powdered. Some stood three feet tall, and were decorated elaborately with ribbons, flowers, jewels, and even replicas of birds and battleships. It usually took hours for a hairdresser to complete the look, which women then wore, without washing their hair, for weeks. In the mornings, a hairdresser or maid would reshape the creation.

THE Victorian Age

DURING the prudish Victorian era of the 1890s, necklines were high and hemlines were low. Ankles, rarely seen, were considered oh-so-sexy. The hourglass figure was a huge trend. Girls and women wore big sleeves and wide skirts to emphasize their small waists. They also wore corsets, which sucked in their stomachs and pushed out their breasts. The corset prevented women from doing much physically—just as well because during the Victorian age, women were considered fragile creatures.

TORTURE DEVICE ALERT: THE CORSET

What is it: an undergarment that pressed in the waist and either flattened or raised the bust, depending on the fashion of the time. The corset, which was made of either metal or whalebones for much of history, was worn until the 1930s—that's a long time to suffer! Sure women could boast of an 8-inch waist, but was it worth all the pain?

THE ROARING
20s

THIS WAS the age of the Flapper—the independent, carefree girl who loved jazz, dancing, and partying, who emerged during the heady days that followed the end of World War I (1914-1918). The Flapper rejected the stifling corset of the Victorian Era and wore tank dresses with dropped waists at the hips. The androgynous look was in, so she bound her breasts to appear as flat as possible. She bobbed her hair to her chin and wore elaborate headbands and turbans. And her legs were daringly uncovered.

THE HAPPY
Homemaker

IN THE 1950s, a trend toward conservatism coupled with a desire to "get back to normal" after World War II, led women back to traditional role models. Above all, the average woman had to be a good wife and a good mother. And she had to look good, too! Cookbooks and advertisements from this time show elegantly made-up women in cocktail dresses or sweater sets and pearls cooking or folding laundry.

© 2004 Jérôme Mireault, colagene.com

did Ya know?

Fashion magazines have been around for hundreds of years. The very first one was launched in England in 1770 and was called the Lady's Magazine. The magazine contained not only the latest fashions, but also poetry and serialized fiction, essays on feminine virtues (such as modesty), advice for moms and wives, recipes, news, and all the latest gossip on the celebrities of the day.

You probably wouldn't be caught dead wearing your mom's clothes—unless she just hit a Marc Jacobs sale! But historically, teens—and children—were dressed like mini-adults. However, with the advent of early rock n' rollers such as Elvis Presley in the '50s, teens became a separate cultural market from their parents. They began to listen to their own music and developed their own fashions, based on their music idols—teen girls took to circular skirts, bobby socks, and ponytails. Boys wore undershirts with rolled up sleeves, tight jeans, and black leather jackets. This fashion divide between parents and the next generation set the scene for the 60s, when teens rebelled en masse and went totally counter culture with the hippie movement of free love, flower power, and experimentation with drugs.

THOSE COLORFUL 80s

LACE GLOVES, mesh shirts, and hair bows made it big thanks to the original Material Girl, Madonna, who made both a music and fashion splash in the mid-1980s. Madonna was also responsible for starting the underwear as outerwear trend (showing your bra) that was popular for a while during the decade. Another hot trend for teens was wearing tight-fitting pants or torn jeans and leg warmers—courtesy of the 1983 hit movie "Flashdance."

SPICE IT UP IN THE 90s

THE NOW-DEFUNCT group The Spice Girls set the tone for the 1990s, influencing a generation of girls to flaunt their bodies with skimpy halter or bustier tops. Kids, especially boys, also started wearing big baggy pants and oversized shirts, a product of both the Seattle-based grunge music scene and the burgeoning hip-hop influence on the culture.

THE 2000s:

IN 2004, most anything goes! Punk mixes with preppy meets bohemian with a touch of hip-hop. Style choices can be difficult in an age of such fashion freedom; just keep in mind that the most important thing is to be comfortable with what you're wearing and true to your own personality. The next chapters will break down the seven hottest styles of the season and give you all the info you need to make them your own.

PREPPY CHIC

EVERYWHERE you go, stores are packed with clothes that shout, "Prep!" And for good reason; the look is clean, neat, and simple, and doesn't take a whole lot of work to pull together.

the LOOK:

- ⦿ button-down shirts
- ⦿ Fair Isle sweaters
- ⦿ short or long sleeved polo shirts
- ⦿ turtlenecks
- ⦿ tweed jackets
- ⦿ khakis, of course!
- ⦿ low-slung, boot-cut slightly flared jeans
- ⦿ pleated and/or plaid skirts
- ⦿ pearls (fake is fine, or borrow Mom's)
- ⦿ nautical anything
- ⦿ loafers
- ⦿ Dr. Scholl's sandals
- ⦿ mocs

© 2004 Jérôme Mireault, colagene.com

15

mad about monograms

Used to be if your name wasn't Muffy or Biff and you didn't have membership at "The Club," you probably didn't own anything with your initials on it. Times have changed, and the monogram is turning up everywhere and anywhere, from Madonna's tush to the Olsen twins' tank tops to J. Lo's sweatshirt.

If you plan on prepping up a T-shirt or sweater with an embroidered monogram, what order do your three initials go in? Preppy protocol demands: The first initial goes on the left, last initial in the middle larger than the other letters, and the middle initial on the right.

L. L. M.

Who's WEARING IT :

- ✓ Hilary DUFF
- ✓ Selma BLAIR
- ✓ Kirsten DUNST
- ✓ Chloe SEVIGNY
- ✓ Lindsay LOHAN
- ✓ And even MADONNA

© Lee Celano/WireImage

Lindsay Lohan

© Jeff Vespa/WireImage

Selma Blair

THE *Background*:

THE PREPPY LOOK evolved from the sporty elegance of the upper class New England private school set. Preppy teens were well heeled, well pedigreed (with at least one relative having arrived on the Mayflower) and were practically guaranteed a spot at an Ivy League College. Girls spoke French, took ballet and tennis, vacationed in Martha's Vineyard, came out at a big debutante ball, and as soon as they turned 16, were given their Mummy's Volvo to drive.

Preppies made the big time in 1980 with the publication of a book that both spoofed and glorified them at the same time, *The Official Preppy Handbook*, which cataloged All Things Preppy. According to the book, Preppies embrace several time-honored values, which include:

- Consistency. Teens were expected to walk, dress, and attend the same schools as their parents and grandparents.

- Nonchalance. Preppies may be loaded, but they don't like to flaunt their money, which explains why girls wear their moms' old Ivy League sweaters.

- Ease. Everything should look easy when done by a Preppy; they should be able to show off their backhand without admitting they took a single lesson!

- Athleticism. They love the expensive equipment almost as much as they do swishing down the mountains, or swimming the laps.

- Discipline. Preps feel good (and please Mummy and Daddy) by studying Latin. That way they'll always have a solid education to fall back on even if their trust fund runs out!

Since the 1980s, the Hardcore Preppy Personality has died out. Instead, preppy fashion has come to be known as a clean, classic look that never really goes out of style.

CLASSIC PREPPY NICKNAMES

Start calling yourself one of these, and you may find yourself automatically reaching for button-downs and polo shirts:

MUFFY, short for any name starting with an "M."

BITSY, this works best if you're petite.

KIKI, a nickname for Katherine, Kathleen, Karen, etc.

BUNNY, for the adorably cute among us.

CORKIE, short for any name starting with a "C" or "K."

"I go to a public school where a lot of the girls dress in baggy or skater clothes. I like my look because not only is it really cute—I just love the collared shirts and pleated skirts—it stands out. I look more like my friends who go to private school.

I also think that dressing preppy makes people assume I'm smart—smarter even than I really am!"

JAMIE, 15

MAKE IT *your Own*

NO ONE said dressing preppy has to be serious or stodgy. Here's how to add some dare and flare to your classic collegiate look:

- Go for shrunken polos and fitted or sheer oxfords instead of the traditional boy-look-alike version.
- Pair preppy with punk by adding a studded belt or silver chain to your pants.
- Go glam with a rhinestone-trimmed belt.
- Find some 50s flare with a bracelet, earrings, or purse adorned with dice or poodles.
- Ditch the traditional turtleneck for a skinny 60s-inspired style.
- Pair your oxford and cardigan with a buckled mini skirt (available in preppy plaid).
- Throw on some high knee socks with your short plaid skirt for a punk-inspired edge.
- Surprise everyone with a pair of shoulder-grazing hoops for some celebrity chic.
- Be bold and ditch the plain T shirt in favor of one with an indie-rocker print.

FASHION MAINTENANCE: CARING FOR
your Sweaters

NEVER separate a preppy from her favorite sweater. Keep your favorites lasting throughout the years by following these tips:

✓ Don't hang your sweaters because they will stretch out. Instead, fold them on a shelf. Or if you're storing them long-term, put them in an unused suitcase.

✓ Don't over-clean. The less you wash them, the longer your sweaters will last. So only clean them when they get really dirty.

✓ Except for cashmere, which needs to be dry-cleaned, hand wash your sweaters in cold water using a mild soap. (You can even throw your wool sweater in the washing machine as long as you use a mild detergent and a low temperature.) After washing, roll the sweater in a towel and gently push on the towel to remove the excess water. Lay it flat to dry.

✓ When washing an Angora sweater, add some salt to the water to prevent the colors in the sweater from running together.

✓ If your sweater gets wrinkled, you can press it with a cool iron.

✓ Remove any pills that accumulate by shaving the surface of the sweater with a razor.

retro prep

The last time the preppy look was this popular was in the late '70s and early '80s.

Here, a comparison between the first preppy generation and the second go-around today:

Then: Lacoste pique knit polo shirt

Now: The croc is still around, but now in more colors and sizes.

Then: Long kilt

Now: Plaid or herring-bone mini

Then: Cotton turtlenecks with cutesy whale, hearts, frogs, or turtle patterns

Now: Belts with whales and alligators on them

Then: Sweater tied around your neck

Now: Sweater tied around your waist

Then: Shop of choice: Brooks Brothers, Talbots

Now: Abercrombie & Fitch, J. Crew

a lady

The preppy look has lately been combined with uber-feminine style (think Chanel's new frayed tweed jackets and Marc Jacobs's skinny pencil skirts). But it's not enough for a preppy girl to be well-dressed; she must be well-mannered, too! Here are some tips on etiquette that'll transform any girl into a lady.

KNOWING WHEN TO ARRIVE

It is not always fashionable to be late. Be on time for all appointments and never keep your host waiting at meal-related gatherings. However, if the party begins in the evening, it is understood that you will arrive later rather than earlier. For any social occasion, always reply to the RSVP.

MEETING AND GREETING

First impressions do count so knowing how to meet and greet anyone, be it your parents' friends or per-spective employers, can win you points for poise! Always offer to shake hands, keep a firm grip, and make eye contact. Another tip? Never answer questions with one word sentences. If you can elaborate on your answer, or better yet, ask a question yourself, you will never be stuck in an awkward situation.

READING THE SILVERWARE

When faced with a dizzying array of forks, knives and spoons, start with the utensils that are farthest from your plate. From your outside left, you'll find your salad fork, then your dinner fork. From your outside right, you'll find your soup spoon, followed by your salad knife, then your dinner knife. The spoon or fork you'll need for dessert is usually at the top of your plate or brought out with the dessert.

ANSWERING YOUR CELL PHONE

The company you are with should be your first priority. If you absolutely must make or take a call, let your friends know first, then step away to do it. Do not stay away for longer than it would take to powder your nose. Never have your cell phone on in a restaurant, a theatre, or any place of worship.

© Nick Leong

PUNK Rock

PUNK ROCK has been around since the 70s, but it's taken decades for the look behind the sound to hit the mainstream fashion world. The style has gone from ratty to glam, with a fusion of enough pinks, plaids and buckles to turn any girl into a hardcore punk princess. But let us warn you: punk rock is not for the faint of heart.

the LOOK:

- studded or zippered jeans
- band T-shirts
- subversive logos like "rock the system"
- asymmetrical striped tops
- cargoes and camouflage gear from your local Army Surplus store
- black skinny pants
- pleated, plaid minis
- well-worn leather or faded jean jackets
- studded belts
- black and white knee-length skirts
- fishnet stockings
- Converse sneakers

© 2004 Jérôme Mireault, colagene.com

21

Who's WEARING IT :

- ✓ Avril LAVIGNE
- ✓ PINK
- ✓ Gwen STEFANI
- ✓ Taryn MANNING

Elvis "proto-punk" Presley took his own brand of country-laced rock and parlayed it into 18 singles that sold over a million copies each between 1956-1960. His hip gyrations were considered so shocking at the time that the "Ed Sullivan Show" would only film him from the waist up!

© George Pimentel/WireImage

Avril Lavigne

Shirley Manson & Gwen Stefani

© Kevin Mazur/WireImage

THE *Background*:

PUNK BURST onto the music scene simultaneously in the U.S. and the UK in the mid-1970s. From the start, the music was angry, rebellious and—most alarming to the public-at-large—anti-authority, with a touch of anarchism. On this side of the Atlantic, musicians, based primarily in New York, rebelled against the overproduced sounds of mainstream rock and the commercialized disco-craze sweeping North America. Across the ocean, middle-class British youths were lashing out against high unemployment rates and what looked like a hopeless, stagnant future. The movement hit its stride with bands like the Clash, the Ramones, and the Sex Pistols, whose subversive songs, such as "Anarchy in the UK" and "God Save the Queen," are now considered quintessential punk rock.

The punk sound was raw and amateurish; the lyrics were repetitious and the songs short. The Ramones, for example, played two-minute songs. Onstage, they could complete an entire set of ten or more songs in a half hour. Punk bands tended to use only a few chords—a fact that led some groups to be deemed "three chord wonders."

But perhaps the most defining characteristics of punk bands were their outlandish and shocking stage antics. Performers were known to shout obscenities, play with their backs facing the crowd, and even vomit onstage and in front of the audience. One singer, Iggy Pop, of the early punk band the Stooges, gained fame for smearing his naked chest with steak and peanut butter and by cutting himself with shards of glass.

Punk was an explosion of energy and rage, and by the early 1980s it had pretty much burned itself out. Ironically, its own success helped kill it. As music producers recognized the commercial value of the sound, they pushed punk into the mainstream, suffocating the amateurish energy of the original movement. However, the punk sound continues to influence bands such as Rancid, Green Day, Good Charlotte, and Blink 182.

a band that will live in Infamy

The biggest, baddest punk group of all was Brit band the Sex Pistols, led by singer Johnny Rotten and bassist Sid Vicious. Johnny Rotten sported spiked hair, ripped jeans, and T-shirts with obscenities on them, and half-sung, half-screamed his songs. Vicious, who had almost no musical training, sometimes performed drunk or on drugs.

The band's first single, "Anarchy in the UK," was released in 1976 and opened with the words "I am anti-Christ; I am an anarchist." Despite being banned by the BBC, the record shot to number one on the UK charts.

In 1978, only two years after its inception, the band broke up. That same year, Vicious was arrested for the murder of his girlfriend, Nancy Spungen. He died of a heroin overdose in 1979 before ever coming to trial.

"I dress punk for two reasons. First, I like the music and, in my free time, go to as many concerts as I can and take pictures. Second, fashion is really important to me. I love the look of checkered Vans, low-slung jeans, a favorite band T-shirt and maybe a black jacket with tons of buckles on it. Dressing that way makes me feel like me."

ANDREA, 18

MAKE IT *your Own*

THE ORIGINAL PUNK LOOK of yesteryear (mid–late 1970s) was radical. Aiming to rock the establishment, youths wore multi-colored Mohawks, pierced their ears and noses with safety pins, and favored ratty, ripped clothes sometimes pulled straight out of trashcans—a far cry from the polished look of such punk princesses as Pink and Avril!

Today, the look is a whole lot less radical and a lot more fashionable. In a nutshell, it's all about being pretty in punk.

- Think black, white, red, and pink in any striped or checked combination. These four colors are the building blocks of punk hues.
- Start with the basics, such as a T-shirt and zippered jeans. If you're feeling bold, go for red and black checked pants or a mini with red or black stockings.
- Sew or safety pin the patches and buttons of your favorite bands to your jacket or jeans.
- Add accessories with an attitude, such as a chain belt and matching necklace, a cabbie hat, pink hoop earrings, a loud tie, and, for a final edgy touch, fingerless gloves. Other accessories that really rock: hip or waist chains, pyramid belts, arm warmers, pink or striped shoelaces, and spiky bracelets and necklaces.
- Select funky, punky footwear by choosing a pair of Converse in any style and color, checkered Vans, combat boots, pointy flats, stiletto heels, and, for around the house, Care Bear slippers (it's called irony).
- To play up your punk rock style on a night out, finalize the look by spiking your hair with gel or molding paste. A layered cut works best, but you can add volume and height with hair clippies and fake hairpieces. For a night out, put on some bright red lipstick and dark eyeliner and you're all set. Even if you never make it to a show, you'd certainly fit in there!

a word on **tattoos** and **piercings**

'Tis true, many punk-inspired fashionistas sport tattoos and/or piercings. Luckily, you can easily get this look pain- and cost-free by wearing henna tattoos and fake piercings. But if your heart is set on getting "the real deal," keep a few things in mind:

- Tattoos are for life. They can be removed by a laser, but the treatment is costly, takes several visits, may be painful, and may not totally erase the image.

- In most states and provinces you have to be at least 18 to legally acquire either a tattoo or piercing.

- Both practices carry a risk of infection (from hepatitis B to HIV) if the instruments are not sterilized or disinfected or are used inappropriately between clients.

- There's also the chance you will have an allergic reaction to the pigments in the tattoos or that your body will "reject" the piercing and the area will become infected.

If you're still interested, here's what to look for in a tattoo or piercing shop:

- The facility is clean and well maintained.

- The practitioner has been trained in preventing diseases transmission and uses disposable needles and gloves for each client.

- All non-disposable equipment is sterilized.

- The tattooist or piercer is happy to answer all of your questions. If, during your interview, you're unsatisfied with an answer, go somewhere else!

FASHION MAINTENANCE:
Keep it clean, kids!

Piercings

FOR THE FIRST three days after a piercing, clean the area two times a day using an antibacterial soap. Make sure your hands are clean. As you clean, gently rotate or twist the jewelry because this helps prevent scabbing. Then pat the piercing area dry with a paper towel.

After three days, clean the piercing once a day for the next several weeks until the piercing seems healed. (Different piercings take different amounts of time, plus every body's different!) If you see any signs of an infection—such as inflammation, redness, or pus—call your doctor.

Tattoos

KEEP A NEW TATTOO covered with a bandage for two hours. Once you remove the bandage, wash the area with antibacterial soap, making sure your hands are clean. Pat the area dry with a clean paper towel. Then apply an antibiotic ointment such as Bacitracin or an A & D vitamin-enriched ointment. Do this for at least twice a day for two to three days.

After five days, you can stop using the antibiotic ointment and switch to a gentle body lotion. Continue to apply it for at least two weeks. Make sure you don't pick or rub any scabbing that occurs. Avoid swimming or exposing the tattoo to sun for several weeks.

© George Crux

did Ya know?

A recent national survey showed that 60 percent of the U.S. population gets their first tattoo or piercing between 15 and 21 years of age.

Goth glamour

GOTHS. YOU'LL KNOW ONE if you see one, and you'll certainly know it if you are one! Goth glamour appeals to the romantic rebel that lurks in all of our hearts, which is why the style continues to survive and even thrive.

the LOOK:

- anything black—black T-shirts, jeans, or skirts
- pants or jeans with chains, zippers, or studs
- flowing skirts
- corset-style tops
- waist cinchers
- romantic vintage dresses
- black leather
- crushed velvet
- black combat boots
- fishnet stockings
- chokers
- medieval-style jewelry
- black fingernails and lipstick

© 2004 Jérôme Mireault, colagene.com

27

the very first goths

Who's WEARING IT :

✓ Liv TYLER
✓ Angelina JOLIE
✓ Kelly OSBOURNE
✓ Amy LEE

No, these guys weren't born in the 1970s. The first Goths lived hundreds and hundreds of years ago. The Goths were ancient Germanic tribes considered barbarians by the Romans. In the fourth century B.C., the Goths moved out of northern Europe and overran the Roman Empire, eventually sacking Rome in 410 A.D.

© Jeff Vespa/WireImage

© Steve Grantz/WireImage

Amy Lee

Kelly Osbourne

28

THE *Background:*

THE GOTH SUBCULTURE was born in England in the late 1970s and early 1980s with an offshoot of punk music that was labeled Gothic, or Goth, even though many of the musicians never chose that label for themselves. Goth rock was characterized by a melancholy sound, morbid subject material, introspective lyrics, and lots of theatrics. Many point to the 1979 song "Bela Lugosi's Dead" by the band Bauhaus as the very first Goth song. Other early Gothic bands include Siouxsie Sue and the Banshees, Joy Division, Sisters of Mercy, and the Cure. The movement soon crossed the ocean and into the United States, where some labeled it "death rock."

By the mid-80s the popularity of Goth music waned, but it was reborn in the late 80s and early 90s with a new generation of bands such as the Mission, the Shroud, Fields of the Nephilim, and Rosetta Stone. Goth morphed into a lifestyle. Young fans took up the Goth banner and become fascinated with All Things mysterious, supernatural, campy or medieval. Following the fashion innovations of their favorite bands, Goths began to adopt the look of black, leather, chains, and heavy eye makeup.

Today, Goth music has branched out into heavy metal and industrial, and it has become difficult for anyone to agree, exactly, on what Goth is beyond 1) a rebellious and artistic spirit and 2) one who has a penchant for wearing black. And many Goths refuse to be labeled at all.

Over the last few years, the Goth subculture has been the target of some criticism. Supposed Goth superstar Marilyn Manson has alienated many with his over-the-top appearance and violent lyrics. The movement was also targeted after the 1999 Columbine High massacre in Littleton, Colorado. The two boys responsible for the slayings were rumored to be Goth because they sported black trench coats and painted their nails black. However, many point out that although Goths love drama, the culture has never been about or condoned violence.

SO WHAT DOES IT MEAN?

Look up "Gothic" in the dictionary and you'll find many different definitions. Here are a few from the American Heritage Dictionary:

- *Of or pertaining to the Goths or their language.*

- *Of or pertaining to an architectural style prevalent in western Europe from the 12th through the 15th century and characterized by pointed arches, rib vaulting, and flying buttresses.*

- *Of or pertaining to a literary style of fiction prevalent in the late 18th and 19th centuries which emphasized the grotesque, mysterious, and desolate.*

- *Barbarous; uncivilized, primitive, crude.*

29

goth:

"People think that dressing Goth is all about wearing black, but it's a lot more than that. I like to paint, and it's a way of letting people know I'm very artistic. I'm also a strong individual and I guess I like to be different from everyone else. I go to a Catholic school and there's only one other Goth girl there besides me.

People also think Goth is about worshipping the devil, but it's really about not being afraid to express your feelings, whether it's happiness or anger. And I have a lot of strong feelings."

AMANDA, 12

MAKE IT your Own

GOTH CAN BE INTIMIDATING, but don't let the look scare you off. Instead, borrow a few elements of this eye-raising style and have some fun with them!

- Think romance. Try a ruffled blouse with flowing sleeves or a shirt adorned with lace. Long, flowing dresses, cinched in the middle, can give you that oh-so-Goth or Medieval look. Having some satin or lace peep out from beneath the hem of your skirt or donning a pair of lacy leggings can add a nice surprise touch.

- Go beyond the basic black. For sure, black is where it's at for a Goth girl, but you can also get away with rich jewel tones such as reds, blues, purples, and greens to bring some bright points of focus to your outfit.

- Be campy. Whether or not you believe in ghosts, goblins, or anything supernatural, there are a lot of tongue-in-cheek accessories to be found, such as spider web tights and skull bracelets and necklaces. Wear them with a smile; irony is the height of Goth fashion.

- Unchain yourself. A lot of Goth fashion revolves around "bondage" gear, such as chokers or dog collars, wrist cuffs, leather straps, garter belts, and chains. But just because you wear a dog collar doesn't mean you're into anything kinky—if you like the look, go for it!

- Borrow from Count Dracula; he knew how to make an entrance! When a hardcore Goth girl goes out at night, she wears a cape (preferably with a rich satin lining). If that's too much drama for you, stick to your leather jacket or try a bolder look with vinyl.

- Walk this way. When you want to give the black boots a rest, try on a pair of pointy-toe shoes or a pair of black sandals. And if you're going to wear tennis shoes, black is best.

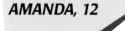

FASHION MAINTENANCE: HOW TO TAKE CARE OF Leather

 **Jackets**

- ✓ Hang your jacket on a hanger with rounded, padded shoulders so the garment will keep its fit.

- ✓ Don't store your jacket in a plastic garment bag as the lack of air may cause it to dry out and lose its softness.

- ✓ If your jacket gets dirty, gently rub the affected area with a damp, clean cloth. If the entire jacket needs to be cleaned, take it to the dry cleaners.

- ✓ Try not to hang your jacket up in direct sunlight as too much exposure can cause the color to fade.

- ✓ Keep your leather jacket in good condition by regularly applying leather cream (most stores that sell leather generally sell this as well).

Boots

- ✓ Rinse off any mud and dirt with water. You can use a sponge, damp cloth, or if the dirt is really sticking, a brush. But go easy on the water because too much can dry and shrink your boots.

- ✓ If your boots get wet, let them air-dry naturally because heat from a fire or heater can harden the leather and cause it to crack. If for some reason they get really soaked, stuff them with newspaper. The paper helps them dry and retains their shape.

- ✓ Regularly condition and waterproof your boots. What product to use and how often to treat your boots may vary depending on the type of boots you own. Talk to a salesperson who can fill you in before you buy a product.

good goth!

It may appear that all Goths look and act the same. But according to those in the know, there are many different types:

- **Baby bats:** Kids who dress in black and listen to Goth bands, but don't know much about the subculture.

- **Spooky kids:** Followers of the shock-rocker Marilyn Manson.

- **Cyber Goths:** Goths who are interested in computers, technology, artificial intelligence, and electronic music such as trance, industrial, and hard-techno.

- **Punk Goths:** Goths who are heavily into the punk scene.

- **Perky Goths:** Girls who like to wear black and listen to Goth music, but don't like the creepy "doom and gloom" aspect of it.

- **Weekenders:** Kids who dress normally during the week but go Goth on the weekends at parties or clubs—also referred to as kids "just going through a phase."

"Dracula" (1931) Actor Bela Lugosi stars as the creepy vampire count.

"Bride of Frankenstein" (1935) Dr. Frankenstein attempts to build a wife for his original monster.

"The Rocky Horror Picture Show" (1975) A campy mock-horror musical that's still a cult favorite today.

"The Hunger" (1983) David Bowie and Catherine Deneuve star as a chic "undead" couple.

"Beetlejuice" (1987) A nice dead couple haunts the family that moves into their house. Winona Ryder stars as an archetypal Goth teen.

"Edward Scissorhands" (1990) Johnny Depp portrays a freakish character with scissors instead of hands.

"Interview with the Vampire" (1994) Tom Cruise and Brad Pitt star as ghoulishly handsome vampires.

"The Crow" (1994) Bradon Lee stars as a young man who returns from the grave possessed by the spirit of a vengeful crow.

Hipster Cool

Chapter 6

IT'S A MOD, mod, mod world when girls combine the hottest looks of the 60s and the 70s with a totally 2004 sensibility! Some of the biggest designers today have reinvented the bell-bottom and the mini, making them so cool you won't even care that your mom wore the same look 20 or 30 years ago.

the LOOK

- miniskirts
- opaque tights
- sleeveless jumpers
- skinny turtleneck sweaters
- hip-slung belts
- bell-bottoms
- knee-high go-go boots
- big earrings
- A-line dresses or skirts
- psychedelic T-shirts or blouses
- halter tops

the moddest TV shows of all time

- "The Avengers" (1961–1969) Characters John Steed and Emma Peel blend wit and style as they fight criminal masterminds.

- "Get Smart" (1965–1970) Don Adams stars as an inept spy Agent 86, along with the very mod Agent 99, a.k.a., Barbara Feldon.

- "The Mod Squad" (1968–1973) Three hip hipsters—Julie, Linc, and Pete— morph from juvenile delinquents into ace undercover agents.

- "Rowan & Martin's Laugh-In" (1968–1973) Goldie Hawn portrays a dippy blonde on this variety show that show-cased the best and worst of some totally swinging hairstyles from the 70s.

- "That '70s Show" (1998–present) Farrah Fawcett haircuts and Tab get a second run in this Fox series.

Who's WEARING IT :

- ✓ Jennifer LOPEZ
- ✓ BEYONCE
- ✓ Samaire ARMSTRONG
- ✓ Geri HALLIWELL

Samaire Armstrong

Beyonce

34

THE *Background*:

AS BOB DYLAN sang 40 years ago, "the times, they are a-changing." That phrase aptly describes the turbulent and idealistic 60s and 70s. On college campuses, students protested the draft and the ongoing Vietnam War. Martin Luther King championed civil rights, and early feminists like Gloria Steinem questioned the unequal treatment of women, igniting new energy in the women's liberation movement. In addition, the birth control pill became widely available, giving women more sexual freedoms and responsibilities than ever before.

The two decades were periods of great idealism but also great disillusionment. The national space program was booming and the United States became the first country to put men on the moon, yet hippies were turning to drugs and free love in protest against an increasingly corrupt world. The nation mourned for the loss of three compelling leaders: John F. Kennedy, assassinated in 1963; Robert Kennedy, assassinated in 1968; and Martin Luther King, also assassinated in 1968. In contrast, Vice President Spiro Agnew and President Richard Nixon resigned amid scandal. The first Earth Day was launched on April 22, 1970, as gas prices soared and the economy went through the worst recession seen in 40 years. And horrifically, National Guardsmen killed four students at Kent State University in Ohio during an anti-war protest.

Fashion was greatly influenced by the politics of the time: miniskirts, for example, were a reflection of the relaxed sexual mores; hippie style borrowed from folk cultures as a gesture non-conformism; and military-wear was appropriated by the youth to protest the government's involvement in the Vietnam War. Setting the standard for years to come, high fashion was determined by the anti-fashion of the streets.

HOW TO WEAR BIG EARRINGS

Big earrings, the rage with the mod set, are back! So wear your big, even gaudy earrings with pride, just don't let them overwhelm you.

- *Skip a necklace. With oversized earrings you don't need any other jewelry around your face. For the same reason, big earrings look great with bare shoulders or a lower cut T-shirt.*

- *Watch the length of the earrings—in general they look best when they graze your shoulders, but go no longer.*

- *If you want to emphasize your cheeks, choose earrings that hit the jawbone. To emphasize your neck, select longer earrings.*

- *Let your locks loose. Big earrings look great when your hair is pulled back, but let a few tendrils hang out around your ears or you may look too severe.*

hipster:

I dress mod because I like to follow the latest trends. And the trend right now where I live is [inspired by] the 60s and 70s. For example, jeans are always in, but now I wear mine with a skinny long neck scarf and a cabby hat. But I have to admit, my style changes a lot depending on what's in. If mod goes out, I'll go with the flow and follow the next trend.

—EDEN, 13

© 2004 Michael Wilhelmi

MAKE IT *your Own*

A FEW STAPLES of the 1960s and 1970s have yet to see a revival—and for good reason. No doubt we can all live without hot pants or 60s-inspired caftans. But the styles that have come back to the fashion frontline are fresh and fun! Here are some tips for looking good and feeling groovy.

- Be bold. Try on combinations of black and white or bright colors. Anything goes—checks, stripes, color blocks or dizzy-making optical art-inspired patterns.

- Make the most of your mini. Balance the short skirt with layers or a more conservative top, such as a crisp white shirt under a sweater or a skinny turtle-neck. If a mini simply isn't you, choose a skirt that ends slightly above or at the knee.

- For a mod finishing touch, pair your skirt with go-go boots (either to the knee or thigh), or if you prefer, a flat heel.

- Find the flare. If big bells are too much for you, go for a more subtle barely there flare.

- Show off those legs. For a total 60s look, wear bold-colored tights with contrasting shoes. Or be really daring and wear bright white tights.

- Open your eyes. False eyelashes were all the rage in the 1960s, but this is one fad you can skip! Instead, flash back to the past with smoky eye shadows and black or brown liquid eyeliner. When it comes to your lips, you'll be feeling groovy with pale, even white, lipstick.

- Keep your locks long. The hippie-inspired long hair parted in the middle is back. So are 60s headbands, which in addition to giving you that retro cool touch, keep the hair out of your eyes quite nicely.

FASHION MAINTENANCE:
How to tie-dye

FLASH BACK to the psychedelic 60s by tie-dying your own shirt.

What you'll need:

- ✓ a cotton or cotton-polyester blend T-shirt
- ✓ fabric dyes in different colors
- ✓ big rubber bands
- ✓ rubber gloves (to protect your hands)
- ✓ large plastic tubs
- ✓ a big spoon

Get going!

- Mix the dyes according to the directions on the box. Use a separate tub for each color. Mix each dye well with a spoon.

- Tie knots in your T-shirt or twist it into sections and tie it up with rubber bands. Don't forget the sleeves!

- Soak your shirt in the dye-mixed lukewarm water for the time indicated on the dye package. If you are using more than one color, start with the lightest color dye and move on to the darkest.

- Remove your shirt from the dye and rinse it well with water until the water runs clear.

- Immerse your shirt in the next tub of dye. Repeat for each color.

- Take off all the rubber bands and/or untie the knots.

- Let your shirt dry.

- Wash it separately the first few times you do the laundry to make sure the excess dye doesn't leak onto any of your other clothes. Machine or hang dry.

the skinny on the **top model** of the 1960s

Her name was Twiggy (real name: Lesley Hornby), and she was famous for being, well, twig-like. At 5' 6" with a super short haircut and stick-straight figure, she looked more like a young boy than a girl, yet Twiggy was the biggest face and figure of the 1960s; she graced the covers of such magazines as Vogue, Newsweek, and Harper's Bazaar. At the height of her popularity, you could find Twiggy tights, dolls, cosmetics, and even lunch boxes.

history of flares

The first group to pull on a pair of bell-bottoms was the US Navy sailors in the 1800s. Bells were practical to wear because the sailors could pull them off quickly in case of an emergency. Then in the 1960s, the look was appropriated by popular pop stars such as Sonny and Cher. The hippies took a shine to bells as well, perhaps because the style seemed counterculture to the straight-legged pants their parents wore.

Bell-bottoms became an even greater hit in the 1970s when the disco craze swept the country. Everyone started wearing huge, flared pants, often in then-techno fabrics like polyester and nylon. After a brief hiatus in the 1980s, boot-cut pants and bell-bottoms reappeared in the mid-1990s, and now they appear to be here to stay.

Why is this look so hot? The flared legs balance out your shape. A-line skirts and dresses, which flare out gently on the sides, are also flattering to figures. Because they don't cling at the hip or the thigh, they will give you a smoother line.

did Ya know?

Yours isn't the first generation to wear hand-braided friendship bracelets. Teens in the 1970s made them out of colored yarns and gave them to their best buddies.

SKATER STYLE

SKATEBOARDING has traditionally been a "guys only" thing, with boys from the cities and suburbs riding handrails and flashing boxers under their big, baggy pants. But today, skateboarding style has merged with surfing and snowboarding culture to evolve into a nationwide fashion trend for girls as well as guys. Call it Street meets Beach.

the LOOK:

- fitted Ts bearing skateboard or surfboard company logos
- short-sleeved "Two-fer" T-shirts with contrasting long sleeves sewn in
- hooded sweatshirts
- Dickies low-rider pants in navy, khaki, charcoal, or black
- flowered bikinis or two-piece bathing suits
- low-slung gaucho shorts or board shorts
- short-sleeve rash guards (even if you never do get in the water!)
- Airwalks, DCs, or any other bulky, big-tongued skate shoes
- beanie hats
- checkered or striped wrist bands
- pullover sweaters
- pastels and Hawaiian prints

surf's UP!

To get yourself in a total surfer girl mood, it's time to check out these classic surfer flicks:

"Gidget" (1959) and "Gidget Goes Hawaiian" (1961)

"Endless Summer" (1966)

"Point Break" (1991)

"Lilo & Stich" (2002)

"Blue Crush" (2002)

"Step Into Liquid" (2003)

Who's WEARING IT :

✓ Mandy Moore
✓ Gwyneth Paltrow
✓ Cameron Diaz
✓ Kate Bosworth

© Jean Baptiste Lacroix/WireImage.com

© Theo Wargo/WireImage

Pro Snowboarder Anne-Flore Marxer

Mischa Barton

THE *Background*

YOU MAY DRESS this way because it's comfy-chic and suits your easygoing lifestyle, but there's a whole history behind the skateboarding phenomenon. Skateboard culture has been going strong for over 40 years. It all started in the 1960s during the era of the Beach Boys when surfing was making a nationwide splash. The first skateboard hit the stores in 1959 and rapidly became a hit with the surfing set. "Sidewalk surfing," as it was called, soon moved from surfers into mainstream teen culture. By 1965, more than 50 million skateboards had been sold.

By the end of the decade, however, the craze suddenly stopped. The clay wheels of early skateboards didn't hug the road well and were hard to maneuver, often causing kids to wipe out. City officials began banning skaters from the streets because the sport was deemed too dangerous. Skateboarding was considered a passing fad, like hula hoops and lava lamps.

But in 1975, a new, improved wheel made out of urethane was created and the skateboard also got wider, which made it more stable to ride. A new generation of kids jump-started the skateboard craze all over again. The first outdoor skate park was created in Florida, and hundreds more were quickly built around the country.

When skate parks began to close in the early 1980s due to insurance liability issues, kids reacted by taking to city streets and abandoned swimming pools to show off their tricks. (Emptied swimming pools were the precursor to today's ramps and half-pipes.) In 1996, when skaters received exposure on the ESPN X Games, the sport boomed. Skateboard shoe manufacturers, such as VANS, began targeting the non-skateboard set and sales soared.

Today, skateboarders like Tony Hawk are household names, and public skate parks are popping up fast and furiously across the country. This look isn't going away any time soon!

from THE MOUTH of a skater:

"I dress this way because I'm an easygoing person and my style reflects my personality. I'm not a girly-girl—the type who freaks if she breaks a nail. I'm casual, relaxed, and a bit of a tomboy."

KATY, 11

41

did Ya know?

THE 'TUDE
BEHIND THE LOOK

The skater image has always had an anti-establishment edge. The average skater, being under 18 and male, and wearing long hair and scruffy, baggy clothes, is often branded a trouble-maker. This "outlaw" image is often inflated by the fact that many skaters living in cities without skate parks take to the streets in search of that perfect grind. And owners of private properties don't want them around. Some cities even view skaters as public nuisances and ban them from public places.

MAKE IT *Your Own*

FORGET THE ULTRA BAGGY look and instead, think comfy chic. Here, some skater girl style tips:

- Layer it! Start with a tank top, pull on a T-shirt, then a long-sleeved shirt, then your hoodie. If you get warm, just start shedding!

- Go Hawaiian. Look for T-shirts in pastels and Hawaiian prints. When you're a surfer girl, life's a beach!

- Perk up your jeans. Buy them embroidered or embroider them yourself for some personal flair.

- Walk in comfort. You can't wear your sneakers everywhere, but you can still be comfortable in flip-flops, leather sandals, and Ugg boots.

- Think truckers. Truly! One hot staple of this look is the mesh trucker hat. Wear it sideways for an old-coot-but-now-cool vibe. One other piece of must-have headwear: a short-billed visor, preferably with a skateboard logo.

- Accent with accessories. Puca shells, once popular in the 1970s, are in again and can add a touch of the beach to any outfit. Put on a pair of cool shades, some Burt's Bees lip gloss, sunscreen (of course), and you'll be ready to hit the streets!

But many would argue that making all kids pay for the crimes of few is discrimination. Skaters are often targeted for just wearing the clothes they wear and listening to the music they prefer. Although Michael Brooke, author of The Concrete Wave: the History of Skateboarding proclaims "Skateboarding represents freedom," it's sometimes a freedom not all skaters can enjoy.

FASHION MAINTENANCE:

If the shoe fits... Wash it!

HOW TO TAKE CARE of your skate sneakers? You can always pop them in the wash, but they may emerge sad versions of their former selves. Instead, try this: Mix up some water and dishwashing soap and soak the shoes in the water for an hour or so. Next, scrub them with a toothbrush or steel wool until they're looking less dingy. Finally, stuff them with newspaper so they will keep their shape and tie them on a coat hanger to dry.

Keep your feet smelling Sweet!

THE LAST THING you want wrecking your image is a major case of smelly feet. Foot odor is caused by bacteria that love to grow in moist, sweaty places like between your toes, under your heel, etc. You can control the odor by

- ✓ washing your feet with an antibacterial soap.
- ✓ making sure your feet are completely dry after bathing and before putting on your socks and shoes.
- ✓ changing your socks after you exercise.
- ✓ wearing sandals and other open-toed shoes that let your feet air out and stay dry.
- ✓ wearing cotton socks. This material absorbs sweat best and will keep you out of stink city!

my belly button's cuter than yours

The skater look usually demands you dare to bare some skin, even if it's just a quarter inch of flesh of your midriff between your wintry pull-over and jeans. And during the summer, skate turns surf with bikinis and cropped tanks galore. But if you're feeling modest or live in a colder climate, you can always throw on a longer T-shirt and higher cut pants. The skater look is totally casual, so feel free to cover up and still look styling.

43

SKATING 101

air: riding with all four wheels off the ground

deck: main platform area of skateboard

fakie: skating backwards

goofy foot: riding with the right foot forward

grind: scraping the trucks (the two parts of the skateboard that connect the deck with the wheels) on a curb or other surface

half pipe: a U-shaped ramp, with a flat section in the middle

heel flip: flipping the board with your heel

manual: a wheelie

nosegrind: grinding only on the front truck

ollie: a jump performed by tapping the tail of the board on the ground—a basic skating trick

railslide: sliding the underside of the board along an object, such as a curb or handrail

tweak: to point the board in a different direction than normal during a maneuver

street skating: skating on streets, curbs, benches and anything else the suburban or urban landscape has to offer

vert skating: skating on ramps or other vertical structures specifically designed for skating

wallie: skating onto, up and over a street object

© 2004 Jérôme Mireault, colagene.com

Boho Grace

PULLING TOGETHER a bunch of eclectic pieces to come up with a polished outfit takes an artistic eye and a flair for fashion. Perhaps that's why bohemian style appeals to the budding artists and writers among us.

the LOOK:

- peasant blouses
- floral prints
- flowing skirts
- camisoles
- vintage clothing
- scarves and shawls
- cardigans
- yoga pants
- leg warmers
- ballet slippers
- berets
- turquoise jewelry

© 2004 Jérôme Mireault, colagene.com

big bucks

Who's WEARING IT :

✓ Kate HUDSON
✓ Mary-Kate and Ashley OLSEN
✓ Jessica SIMPSON
✓ Ashlee SIMPSON

for advertisers, that is. In 2002, teens age 12-19 doled out more than $170 billion on clothing, shoes, and accessories, according to Teenage Research Unlimited. With teens spending more time in malls than any other age group, adolescents are definitely considered a hot market. But don't be afraid to step away from the hype. As every boho-gal knows, the best fashion finds are hidden off the beaten paths in vintage and second-hand stores. And you can be sure that you'll never catch anyone else in the same outfit!

Ashlee Simpson

Mary-Kate and Ashley Olsen

THE *Background:*

THE WORD BOHEMIAN has come to mean someone with artistic or literary interests who shuns a conventional life. How did this definition evolve?

First of all, there is actually a place called Bohemia. Bohemia was a part of the Holy Roman Empire, and for a while it was considered a distinct kingdom within the empire. Presently, it is a region of the Czech Republic that includes the capital city, Prague.

Bohemia is often mistakenly thought to be the homeland of the Gypsies, (also known as the Romany)—bands of nomads that have wandered Europe since the 14th or 15th century. Over time, because of this misconception, "bohemian" came to describe anyone who was free, independent, and cared little for material goods.

The word cropped up occasionally in the mid-1800s in the works of French authors such as George Sand and Honoré de Balzac. Then in 1848, a relatively obscure Parisian poet, Henry Murger, wrote a series of sketches called *Scènes de la Vie de Bohème*. The book describes the loves, studies, amusements, and sufferings of a group of artists living in the Latin Quarter of Paris. The sketches were brought to the stage in Paris in 1849, and the play became a huge hit. Since that point, the definition of the word bohemian has been sealed.

A BOHEMIAN IN PARIS

The early bohemians who made their home in the Latin Quarter of Paris in the 19th century were often the poorest of the poor. However, the struggling writers, painters, sculptors and composers shaped their impoverishment into a wellspring for their work. Their poverty became an artistic statement, forming an avant-garde movement that embraced "art as all."

Fashion, to the early bohemians, was influenced by both their poverty and their artistry. Their mishmash dressing style was often seen as eccentric and interpreted as an anti-fashion statement. Modern bohemian style has inherited these qualities and taken on the flavors of other countercultures, too, such as the hippies and the Beat Generation.

from THE MOUTH of a

bohemian gal:

"I love to wear vintage clothes from the 50s, 60s—almost any era! For example, I might wear jeans with a skirt over it, a thrift store shirt, and a 50s-style sweater. I don't dress like everyone else, and kids are always telling me I look cool and interesting. I think I have a flair for fashion and love combining different looks. I hope one day to become a fashion designer."

–GABRIELLE, 13

Red Copper © Matt Bowden

MAKE IT *your Own*

GOING BOHEMIAN means taking pieces from different eras and styles and putting them together to create a unique statement. Some helpful hints:

- Isn't it romantic? Add some soft, feminine pieces, such as ruffled blouses or skirts, or T-shirts edged with lace, to your wardrobe. Shirts with embroidery or appliqués also fit the look.

- Think Gypsy. Peasant blouses, while passé in some fashion circles, always work for the bohemian girl. Pair them with beaded ethnic necklaces for some true retro class.

- Clash, baby, clash. Pairing stripes with checks or floral patterns is *très artistique*, and shows off your individualistic flair. Add colorful socks, tights, or 80s-inspired leg warmers as a final creative touch.

- Go for comfort. Bohemian gals don't have to worry about wobbling on stiletto heels. Flat is where the look is at. If you're not into ballet slippers, opt for flat-soled boots or Birkenstock-like sandals.

- Mix in rugged pieces. Too much femininity can be over-powering, so throw a denim jacket over your floral dress, or mix up the look by wearing combat boots.

- Everything in moderation. Vintage pieces stand out most when worn with something new. Add a vintage brooch or earrings to your black T and jeans. Or pair that 50s cardigan with a pair of cargo pants.

- Think Asian. You'll feel comfortable yet totally Zen in a kimono-influenced top or a pair of karate-style pants.

- Beat up isn't bad. Jeans with holes, ripped shirts, or partially unraveled scarves give you that "Hey, I'm too busy creating my next masterpiece to care about my clothes" vibe.

- Leave your brush at home. Complete your look with a disheveled hairstyle that looks like you have more important things to think about than hair. Put on a little bit of lipgloss and you're good to go!

FASHION MAINTENANCE:

SECOND-HAND STORES offer fabulous clothes—often designer—at great prices. But before you buy, check out these vintage shopping tips:

- Buy for quality, not price. You'll find some great deals while vintage shopping, but don't forget that the important point is to love the piece and plan on wearing it constantly.

- Examine the garment carefully. Avoid buying anything with an unfixable problem, such as cigarette burns, large holes, stained armpits or a stained lining. As well, do a thorough button check to make sure that a one-of-a-kind button isn't missing.

- If you buy a vintage garment made before 1972, there won't be a care label. In 1972, the Federal Trade Commission created its *Care Labeling Rule*, requiring manufacturers to label clothing with at least one safe method to clean the garment. If your vintage piece is missing a care label, and you're not sure you can throw it in the washer, play it safe by first taking it to the dry cleaners and asking for advice on how to clean it.

- Check the shoulders to make sure the fabric isn't stretched out of shape from being on a hanger for so long.

- Head to the dressing room. Don't be thrown off by sizing. Today's sizes have little bearing on those from yesteryear. A size 12 from the 1960s could be a size 6 today. The only way to know for sure if it fits you is to try it on.

- If you're buying vintage from online auction sites such as eBay, make sure to ask questions about the garment's measurements, quality, and wear. Also make a point of buying from sellers with good reviews and good return policies. Sometimes what you see on your computer screen may not be what you get!

- Don't expect to find anything. Vintage shopping can be very time consuming and its rewards can be inconsistent. Instead of having a specific item in mind, be open to surprises, try on the outrageous, relax and have fun!

match your figure with an era

This decade-by-decade guide will help you find a figure-flattering outfit:

- If your waist is wide, go for a flapper-era dropped waist from the 1920s.

- To emphasize a small waist, try a full skirt with a waistband, popular in the 1930s.

- Balance broad hips by wearing a jacket with shoulder pads from the 1940s.

- Show off your nice bust with a snug sweater set from the 1950s.

- Play down your thighs with an A-line skirt from the 1960s.

- Flaunt your pretty shoulders with an off-the-shoulder, asymmetrical shirt from the 1980s.

Bring out the romantic in you by watching the following movies, named the "Top 10 Most Romantic Movies of All Time" according to a poll of directors, writers, actors and other filmmakers conducted by the American Film Institute.

1) Casablanca (1942) starring Humphrey Bogart and Ingrid Bergman.

2) Gone with the Wind (1939) with Clark Gable and Vivien Leigh.

3) West Side Story (1961) with a beautiful and young Natalie Wood.

4) Roman Holiday (1952) starring Gregory Peck and Audrey Hepburn.

5) An Affair to Remember (1957) with Cary Grant and Deborah Kerr.

6) The Way We Were (1973) starring Robert Redford and Barbra Streisand.

7) Doctor Zhivago (1965) with Omar Sharif and Julie Christie.

8) It's a Wonderful Life (1946) with Jimmy Stewart and Donna Reed.

9) Love Story (1970) starring Ali McGraw and Ryan O'Neal.

10) CityLights (1931) with Charlie Chaplin and Virginia Cherrill.

Fly-girl Flair

WHETHER OR NOT you can tell Dr. Dre (rapper and producer) from Dr. J (basketball star), hip-hop is here to stay. This look has moved from the urban underground and steamrolled the suburbs. In the process, what used to be a macho subculture has opened up to fly-girls and Missy wannabes everywhere.

the LOOK:

- velour/terrycloth tracksuits
- jumpsuits
- brightly colored jerseys sporting brand or team names
- hoodies
- loose-fitting jeans or low-slung hip-huggers
- high-end tennis shoes or Timberland boots
- gold monogrammed belts and/or necklaces
- baseball caps, do-rags or bandannas
- newsboy caps
- big hoop earrings

© 2004 Jérôme Mireault, colagene.com

totally phat classic rap hits of the **80s** and **90s**

"I Feel For You", 1984, Chaka Khan

"Walk This Way", 1986, Run-D.M.C.

"Fight for Your Right to Party", 1986, Beastie Boys

"Push It", 1987, Salt-N-Pepa

"Wild Thing", 1989, Tone Loc

"Bust a Move", 1989, Young MC

"Ice Ice Baby", 1990, Vanilla Ice

"Baby Got Back", 1992, Sir Mix-A-Lot

"Hip Hop Hooray", 1993, Naughty By Nature

"Gangsta's Paradise", 1995, Coolio

"Can't Nobody Hold Me Down", 1997, Puff Daddy

Who'S WEARING IT :

✓ EVE
✓ Mary J. BLIGE
✓ Missy ELLIOTT
✓ Christina AGUILERA

© Theo Wargo/WireImage

EVE

© Steve Grantz/WireImage

Missy Elliott

THE *Background* :

HIP-HOP culture was born in the late 1970s, primarily in the Bronx neighborhood of New York City, and combined rapping, break dancing, and tagging, or graffiti. All three "urban arts" reflected the nitty-gritty of ghetto life and quickly influenced the way inner city kids talked, gestured, and dressed.

Rap music, the most recognized aspect of hip-hop culture, has its roots in Jamaican "toasting," the practice of DJs giving shout-outs to the crowd and introducing a song before spinning the record. The shout-outs and speeches evolved over time, incorporating rhyme and rhythm, to the point where the DJ's performance became the focus of a party. DJs would play their turntables like instruments, interrupting or prolonging the music and beat by placing a finger on the record, then scratching it back and forth to suit their lyrics.

One of the first rap records debuted in 1979 with the Sugarhill Gang's "Rapper's Delight". The music quickly spread from New York City to black neighborhoods throughout the United States. Mid-decade, rap began to cross over to the white suburban population as rap artists increasingly sampled from more mainstream rock songs and white musicians, such as the Beastie Boys, began to embrace the form. Run-D.M.C.'s rap remake of Aerosmith's rock hit "Walk This Way," was on the first rap album to hit the Pop Music Chart's Number Ten.

Today, hip-hop is everywhere with the success of artists such as Missy Elliot; Beyonce; Eminem, whose album The Marshall Mathers LP sold nearly two million copies in its first week of release; and OutKast, whose album Speakerboxxx/The Love Below won album of the year at the 2004 Grammys. In fact, hip-hop is the second most preferred genre of music, second only to rock. Advertising, movies and television all hype hip-hop, allowing many hip-hop artists such as Queen Latifah to branch out into lucrative acting careers.

did Ya know?

HOW BREAK DANCING BEGAN

Break dancing was also born on the streets of New York City in the 1970s. Kids would gather on street corners and try out moves they adapted from the TV show "Soul Train," singer Michael Jackson's robot-like gyrations, and kung fu movies.

Break dance "crews" met at certain corners or subway stations and challenged each other to dance-offs. They formed circles where two dancers at a time would compete, matching each other move for move until one outperformed the other. Break dancing eventually moved from the streets to the clubs and into mainstream American culture.

Graffiti, in some shape or form, has been around since early man scrawled pictures and symbols inside cave walls. But the first modern-day taggers were teens from De Witt Clinton High in the Bronx in the 1970s, according to hip-hop historian Nelson George. Clinton High was conveniently located near a Transit Authority yard where out-of-service subway cars were stored. Students, armed with spray paint and felt-tipped pens, set to decorate the cars with their own brand of urban art. Because graffiti was illegal, they signed their work with "tags," or fake names, so no one could trace the artwork back to them.

MAKE IT *your Own*

HIP-HOP STYLE is one of the fastest growing segments of the fashion industry. Artists such as Sean "P. Diddy" Combs, Jay-Z, and Russell Simmons, the founder of Def Jam Records, have even kick-started their own clothing lines (Sean John, Rocawear and Phat Farm, respectively). The style is sleeker and more sophisticated than the ultra-baggy pants and hoodies of yesteryear. And while the look was originally more a "guy thing," fashion designers are quickly recognizing the popularity of hip-hop among females. Today's tenets of hip-hop style:

- Comfort comes first. Jeans fit loosely rather than skintight. But not everything has to be baggy. Pair a tight T-shirt with loose bottoms for a totally fly look.

- You can't have too much of a good thing. Match your hat to your sweatshirt to your T-shirt to your track pants.

- Name brands rule. If you have a favorite brand, such as Tommy Hilfiger, FUBU, Karl Kani or Rocawear, feel free to flaunt it large and loud. The same goes with parading the name of your city's professional sports teams.

- Color is cool. There's nothing drab about hip-hop apparel; the style celebrates the energy and power of rap and funk, and therefore demands vivid colors— fuchsias, oranges, yellows, deep reds and blues.

- Clean's the scene. Save the muddy, dirty tennis shoes for hiking or running. When it comes to walking around town, keep those Nikes or Reeboks unsmudged. They should look like you just bought them off the store display.

- Gold's your best friend. No hip-hop look is complete without a little bit of bling bling around your neck or wrist. Twenty-four karat stuff is always nice, but faking it's fine, too.

graffiti-3 © Nick Cowie

FASHION MAINTENANCE: TREATING YOUR
Bling Bling RIGHT !

IF YOU'RE LUCKY ENOUGH to own gold, silver or precious stones, you'll want to keep them in good condition. Here's how:

- ✓ Wrap each piece of jewelry in a piece of fabric or in a separate compartment of your jewelry box. Otherwise it may get scratched.
- ✓ Take off your jewelry when swimming because chlorine can damage gold and certain stones.
- ✓ Avoid leaving precious stones on a window sill or any other place that receives a lot of sunlight as certain gemstones, such as amethyst or rose quartz, may fade.
- ✓ Store beaded necklaces flat. Hanging them can stretch them.
- ✓ Periodically check the prongs of your jewelry to make sure they aren't loose. You could lose the stone!
- ✓ Store silver pieces in airtight plastic bags to prevent tarnishing. If your silver is tarnished, scrub it with a toothbrush and toothpaste. Surprisingly, this gets rid of the grime.

from THE MOUTH of a

fly-girl:

"I like to wear a baggy, hip-hop style in part because I love rap music. The way I dress reflects my choice in music. Also, most of the kids at my school dress skater-style. Now that's comfortable, but hip-hop is even more comfortable and that's important to me … And I like the fact that I have my own style and am not afraid to look a little different from most people."

MORGAN, 11

A bad rap?

The most notorious form of hip-hop music is gangsta rap, which evolved in the 1980s and early 1990s with the likes of N.W.A., Snoop Dogg, the late Tupac Shakur, the late Notorious B.I.G., and, more recently, 50 Cent. Gangsta rap, such as 50 Cent's chart-topping "P.I.M.P.", depicts violence, drugs, and sex, using lyrics that contain explicit obscenities.

Gangsta rappers are often criticized for serving as poor role models to their young listeners. Many question the value of the rappers' brutal depictions of the ghetto, sexist portrayal of women, and negative stereotypes of black culture.

Defenders of gangsta rap however, argue that the music accurately portrays inner-city life, thus giving the artists a way to express themselves and educate others about the injustices faced by those in their positions.

Rappers such as Public Enemy Number One and N.W.A. are known for using their music as a political statement.

It is important to note however, that not all hip-hop performers use foul language and sexual or violent imagery. Some rappers even use their celebrity status to fight violence. Missy Elliott, for example, serves as the national spokeswoman for Break the Cycle, a non-profit group aimed at preventing domestic violence.

WASH & WEAR

HERE ARE SOME TIPS on everything you need to know, from A to Z, on looking your best and feeling good in your own skin.

- acne
- bras
- cellulite
- skin types
- eating disorders
- figure flattering clothes
- face shapes
- job interviews
- makeup
- nutrition
- perspiration
- stain removal
- UVB/UVA Protection
- vanity sizing
- zippers

cne

PRETTY MUCH every gal gets a pimple or blackhead now and then. To control breakouts, wash pimple-prone areas with warm water and mild soap two times a day. Remove any excess oil after washing by dipping a cotton ball in astringent or toner and gently wiping it over trouble spots. Make sure you select noncomedogenic (non acne-forming) makeup and wash off any makeup every night before going to sleep. You might also want to talk to your dermatologist about the different products on the market that can help combat acne, from benzoyl peroxide to Retin-A.

Bras

Experts say that 70 per cent of us are wearing the wrong-sized bra. Find your true size with a little bit of measuring and mathematics.

STEP 1: Take a tape measure and measure around your chest just under your breasts. (ß)

Step 2: If your measurement is 33 inches or under, add 5 inches to that number. If your measurement is over 33, add 3 inches.

STEP 3: Round up until you get an even number. (For example, if you come up with 35, round up to 36). This is your band size—the number part of the bra size (30, 32, 34, etc.)

STEP 4: To find your cup size, measure over the biggest point of your bust line. (A)

STEP 5: Subtract your band size from this number. The difference between this measurement and your band size is your cup size. If it's 0, you are a double A cup. One inch means you're an A cup, two inches a ß cup, three inches a C cup, and so on.

For example, if your band size was 36 and you measure 38 inches around the fullest part of your chest, your bra size is 36ß.

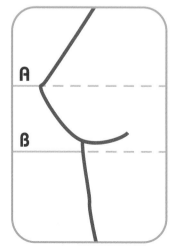

Cellulite:

Got a little? Not to worry. Almost everyone does. And despite what you read, there's no product that will magically make it disappear. Cellulite is simply ordinary fat that develops below the buttocks. The best way to control it is to eat a well-rounded, low-fat diet and get regular exercise.

Combo skin

You have combination skin if your face tends to be dry on your cheeks but oily in the T-zone—across your forehead, down your nose, and around your mouth. The trick to manage combo skin is to use a moisturizer, but only on those areas of your face that need it. On oily areas, use tissue paper to blot extra oil during the day.

Dry skin

Keep your skin looking and feeling smooth by limiting how often you wash your face (twice a day is enough) and using warm, not hot, water; cleaning and hot water both rob your skin of its natural oils. Choose a super fatted soap and apply moisturizer after washing your face.

Eating disorders

THE SAD TRUTH is as many as 10 million women and girls are battling eating disorders such as anorexia (when girls restrict their food intact and lose excessive amounts of weight) or bulimia (when girls overeat, then purge through vomiting, laxative use, or over-exercising). You can avoid this destructive disease by questioning the "thin is in" culture that surrounds us and realizing that it's better to be healthy and happy than obsessively scrutinizing every little calorie you consume.

Keep in mind that while we look to the celebs as our standards of beauty, most are severely under-weight compared to the average woman. And, when you see a star's photo in a magazine, her body has often been digitally altered to appear even thinner than she really is! So don't believe everything you see. (Also see Vanity sizing.)

Figure flattering clothes

The best rule of thumb: If you feel comfortable in an outfit, you probably look good in it, too. This said, here are a few tips to keep in mind: Jackets and sweaters that hit your waist or knees are generally more flattering than those that hit your hips or thighs. Pants and skirts with a flare help balance out your figure. And low-waisted pants are great for making your derriere look smaller. If you'd like a boost in the chest department, high-neck shirts will make you look a little bustier.

Heart-shaped face

MAKE THE MOST of your face shape by wearing long side-swept bangs to balance a wide forehead and a narrow chin. As for glasses, go for Aviator frames or frames that are wider at the bottom than top. PS: Not sure which face shape you are? Simply pull your hair back, look into the mirror, and trace the outline of your face with your finger, a bar of soap, or even lipstick.

Job interviews

Putting your best face forward in a job interview will definitely increase your chances of success! Experts say that 55% of the impression you make on an interviewer comes from your appearance. Some tips: Limit your makeup, jewelry, and perfume. Make sure your hair, teeth, and nails are clean. In terms of what to wear, err on the conservative side, regardless of the company's actual dress code. Smile, sit up straight, and remember to make eye contact.

Long face

A SHORT CUT will help make your face look shorter, as will a side part versus a center one. Soft bangs cut above the eyebrows will also complement your look. As for glasses, large round frames that contrast and soften the shape of your face are the ticket!

Ready to go © Jana Werner

Smile

60

Makeup

Your natural beauty is all you need to shine! This said, playing with a little makeup can be fun—just use a light hand. On a night out, try a touch of lip gloss, some shimmery eye shadow, and maybe a dash of mascara. Remember, unless you're in a totally Goth or punk mode, the key to make-up is making it look like you're not wearing any!

Nutrition

You are what you eat—and nutrition affects your looks, too. Stay healthy and happy by eating well-balanced meals consisting of fruits and vegetables, dairy products, grains, such as pasta, and protein found in meats, peanut butter, and fish. And don't forget to drink lots of water! Water helps to flush your body of toxins and keeps you hydrated, making your skin soft and supple.

Oval-shaped face

MOST ANYTHING goes if your face is oval—in fact, this shape is considered the "ideal" face shape! So select whatever hairstyle you like—from a closely cropped cut to long, long layers. Ditto for glasses.

Perspiration

Arm yourself against underarm sweat with an anti-perspirant or deodorant. What's the difference? Antiperspirants temporarily contract the sweat glands in your armpits, thus blocking perspiration from reaching the surface of the skin. Deodorants simply cover up B.O. with a fragrance.

If you choose to use an antiperspirant, remember that sweating is natural: it's your body's way of cooling off. Some doctors believe that wearing antiperspirants while playing sports, or other activities that cause a normal amount of sweat, can be dangerous.

Round-shaped face

LAYERS OR CHOPPY bangs will complement your face shape. As will hair that is chin-length or longer. When choosing glasses, go for square frames that nicely counterbalance the contours of your face.

Square-shaped face

LAYERS LOOK GREAT with your face shape, and so do curls, which balance out the boxiness of your face. If you need to choose a pair of frames for your glasses, oval shapes will complement your look nicely.

Stain removal

Spilled something on your favorite shirt or sweater? Here are some home-grown remedies you can try: Remove ink with hair-spray; chewing gum with ice; lipstick with vegetable oil; blood with a handful of salt and cold water; and ketchup with a mixture of white vinegar and water. PS: The key to getting rid of a stain, whatever it may be, is to treat it ASAP, before it has time to set.

UVB/UVA Protection

One thing you never want to do is face the sun alone. Dermatologists recommend wearing sunscreen each and every day—not just when you hit the beach or the slopes!

When choosing a sunscreen, opt for one with at least a Sun Protection Factor (SPF) of 15. SPF screens out ultraviolet ß rays—rays that cause sunburn and some kinds of skin cancer. The higher then SPF, the longer time you can spend in the sun before you'll burn. For example, if your skin normally burns in 10 minutes, an SPF of 4 would give you 40 minutes in the sun before burning. An SPF of 15 will give you 150 minutes. But keep in mind that if you sweat or swim, you'll need to reapply sunscreen more frequently!

And make sure your sunscreen gives you broad-spectrum protection, which also filters out ultraviolet (UVA) rays—the ones that can cause melanoma, a deadly skin cancer.

Vanity sizing

ARE YOU HAVING trouble determining your size when you try on clothing? You're not the only one. It's all due to a new trend in the fashion industry known as "vanity sizing." Fashion marketers reckon that the better we feel about our bodies, the more we'll be willing to buy. As a result, clothing manufacturers are dummying down sizes to give us the impression of having smaller figures, playing up the predominant myth that skinny equals happiness.

One recent study conducted at the University of North Texas examined over 1,000 different types and brands of women's pants and found that one brand's size 10 was another brand's size 6! The more expensive the brand, the more likely it was to be vanity-sized. So just remember, don't get hung up on the size of the jeans you fit into; how you look—and feel—in them is much more important.

Zippers

Stuck? Rub a bar of soap on your zipper to grease up the metal teeth and it should start moving freely. And what if your zipper tends to slide down? Some swear that if you spray hairspray on the zipper after washing it, the zipper will stay in place until the next washing.

Conclusion

What dictates fashion? Everything and anything.
FASHION DESIGNERS have a large say in what we wear. But some of their creations—high fashion or "haute couture"—pushed by fashion mags, store buyers, and the ultra-rich are so expensive and out-there that they rarely make it into the mainstream.

Celebs also carry a lot of weight. A couple years ago, Avril Lavigne's early rocker-girl persona helped popularize punk. In the 1980s, Madonna's racy outfits started a trend of half-dressed girls. At the same time, Princess Diana, the former Princess of Wales, set the standard for elegance and style for girls and women around the world.

Movies and television influence our choices as well. After *Men in Black* came out in 1997, there was a surge in Ray-Ban sales. The Matrix films popularized the long, black trench coat. And "Dawson's Creek" put preppy back on the fashion map.

The most important player in the game of fashion however, is you. Style is not something to be learned by rote, and *Fearless Fashion* is not a manual. Rather, take these looks, these ideas, these tips, and make them your own. Build on them. Style is creating your own look, your own attitude.

And don't forget, it's okay to be fickle. If one month you're a total prep and the next you find yourself eyeing corsets and skull rings, not to worry. With confidence, you can pull off any style at any time. Mixing up your look is what fearless fashion is all about! The best fashion trend is to be true to yourself.